What Can You Expect from *The Fire Writer*?

If you want to instill a love for writing AND for hearing the voice of God, Lauren Stinton's *The Fire Writer* is just what you need. Lauren taught creative writing at our homeschool co-op and EVERY student, boy/girl, young/old, did NOT want to miss that class. She will stir their creativity, help open their hearts to hear the voice of God, and she may even help YOU hear Him a little better too! Lauren creates beautiful pictures with her words that will have you longing to know Jesus and definitely looking for more of her books to read. I'm 53 and I'm always waiting for the next one in her Hamal series.

– Jilann Carlson, Arrows Homeschool Co-op

Lauren has done an amazing job of crafting a tool building solid writing skills while being entertaining and engaging for students of all ages. The unbelievable part is that she does this while having the student connect with God in an immersive experience, challenging the student to use all their senses while completing the assignment. I completed a couple of these assignments myself and I was impressed. You will be too. This is a one-of-a-kind writing curriculum for your students.

– Jennifer Stapleton, M.A. CCC-SLP, former educator and curriculum writer

Lauren has a powerful gift in activating others into their fullness. As I partake in the writing exercises, I am never disappointed in the ways in which the Holy Spirit infuses my writing with His Divine Plans. There are plenty of books addressing the technical details of writing. Radiance is a breath of fresh air in partnering with the Holy Spirit to activate the solutions we are each called to bring to the world. We need more than technique in these days; we need fresh, God-breathed solutions. Enjoy this work with your family and let it activate, inspire, and empower you to seize the Kingdom of God and pull it down to earth.

– Crystal L. Clark, homeschooling lioness, mom of four

When the gifted imagination of the writer, Lauren Stinton, and her passion to explore new ways to manifest the kindness of our Creator come together, the result is a novel called Radiance and this workbook. This book has the potential to do for our generation what C. S. Lewis's books did for his. It is just that heart-warming!

– Rochelle Holben, director, Elijah House

Using this beautiful story of a child discovering the depths of a relationship with God, Lauren invites children (of all ages) to explore how God is speaking and to marry their spirituality with creativity. This marriage is an essential one for the future of any civilization, and when it starts early, it sets a person on a path of abundant life that changes them and many others through them. Lauren has clearly allowed this marriage in her own life, and I am grateful that she has created a path for others to join her on this journey, where the voice of God, our imagination, and our creativity draw us into new experiences with Him and new understanding of the world we live in!

— John E. Thomas, president, Streams Ministries

THE FIRE WRITER

Hearing God's Voice Through Creative Writing

A COMPANION GUIDE TO

RADIANCE

LAUREN STINTON

The Fire Writer: Hearing God's Voice Through Creative Writing

Copyright © 2020 by Lauren Stinton

Calligraphy by Carla Stinton

Cover design and layout by Trace Chiodo
www.tracechiodo.com

All rights reserved. No part of this book, except for small excerpts for review or teaching purposes, may be reproduced or transmitted in any form without prior written permission from the author.

Unless otherwise marked, Scriptures are taken from the NEW AMERICAN STANDARD BIBLE®, Copyright © 1960, 1962, 1963, 1968, 1971, 1972, 1973, 1975, 1977, 1995 by The Lockman Foundation. Used by permission.

Scripture quotations marked NLT are taken from the *Holy Bible*, New Living Translation, copyright © 1996, 2004, 2015 by Tyndale House Foundation. Used by permission of Tyndale House Publishers, Inc., Carol Stream, Illinois 60188. All rights reserved.

Printed in the United States of America

ISBN 978-1-7321216-3-8

Scenes from the *Radiance* book by Lauren Stinton are a work of fiction. Names, characters, places, events, and incidents are either the products of the author's imagination or used in a fictitious manner. Any resemblance to actual persons, living or dead, or actual events is purely coincidental.

Visit
www.thehamalbooks.com
to learn more about Radiance and her world

Visit
www.laurenstinton.com
for more information about the author

Other books by Lauren Stinton

The Hamal Books:
Radiance
Should I Choose to Die Again
The One-Eyed Man
The Healer Who Didn't Remember
www.thehamalbooks.com

The House of Elah series:
The House of Elah
The Alusian's Quest
The King's Man

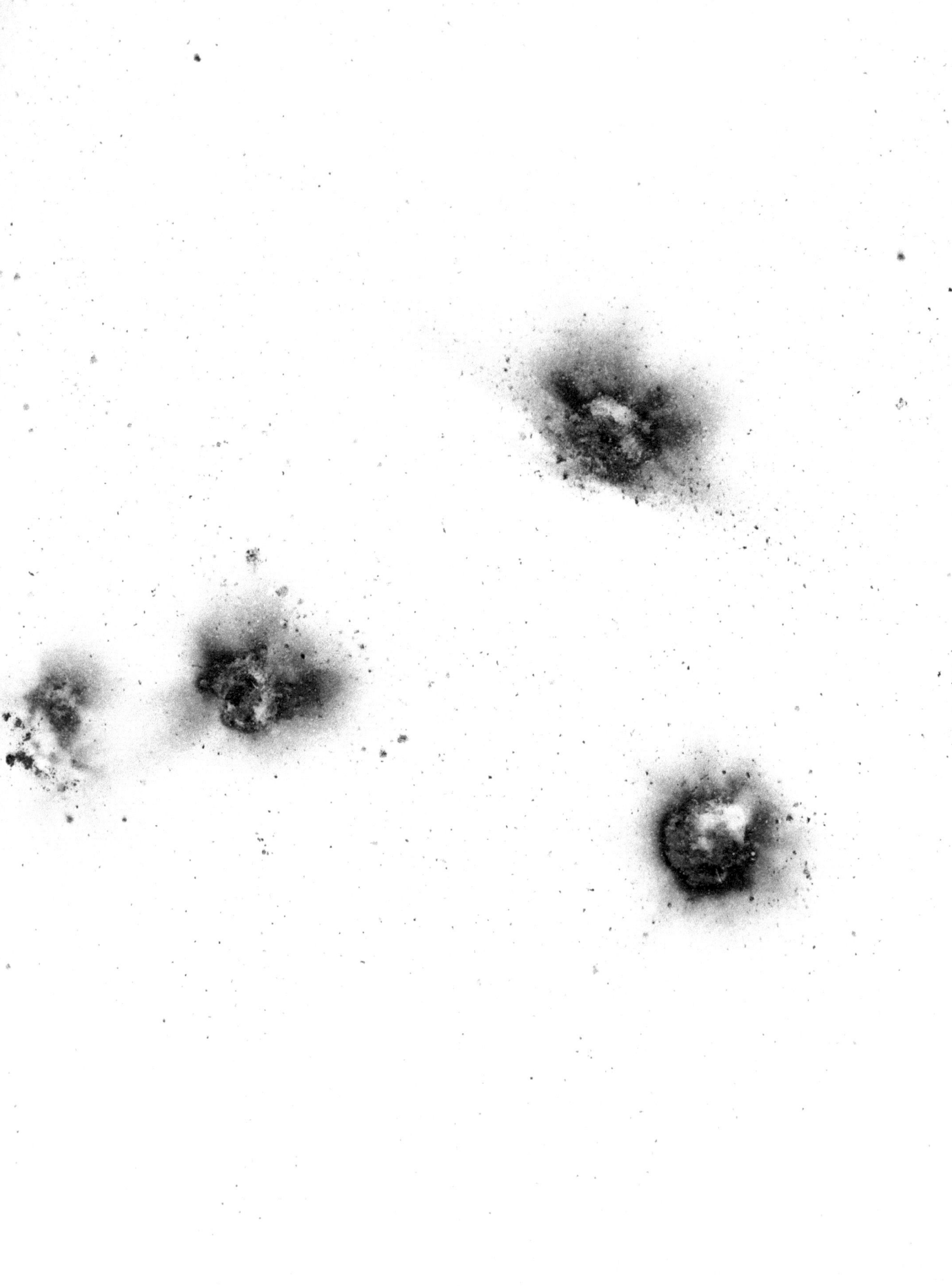

TABLE OF CONTENTS

A Note to Parents	11
How to Use This Book	13
Lesson Plan	15
Fire Lesson 1	21
Fire Lesson 2	27
Fire Lesson 3	33
Fire Lesson 4	37
Fire Lesson 5	43
Fire Lesson 6	49
Fire Lesson 7	55
Fire Lesson 8	61
Fire Lesson 9	67
Fire Lesson 10	73
Fire Lesson 11	79
Fire Lesson 12	85
Fire Lesson 13	91
Fire Lesson 14	97
Fire Lesson 15	103
Evaluating Your Child's Work	111
World Map	116

A NOTE TO PARENTS

As I prepared to write this book, I realized I didn't want to write a "teaching book." The world is filled with teaching books—many of them on writing—and honestly, the idea of trying to teach young people how to craft good sentences doesn't excite me. I prefer writing stories. Getting straight to the point.

So this isn't *just* a book about writing. It is also meant to help children practice seeing and hearing Jesus.

Or Ruwok, as Radiance calls him.

This companion guide will help you and your child connect with Jesus through creative writing. Neither of you needs to be overly experienced with writing, and the guide can still be used even if you aren't sure what the Creator's voice sounds like. This guide is for *practice*, so hopefully by the time you and your child are finished, you'll know more about his voice than you did at the beginning.

As you go through this companion guide, may you and your child come to know the Creator's heart at a deeper level—from fire to fire.

Lauren
(and Radiance)

HOW TO USE THIS BOOK

This guide contains fifteen creative writing exercises and the excerpts from *Radiance* that accompany them.

If you're leading a young child through the writing exercises, read each lesson aloud, and then help your child complete the exercise. I encourage you to do the exercise as well and have fun "comparing notes" with your child. (Obviously, one of you will need to use a separate notebook.)

Time suggestions: The 15-minute time suggestions are more like guidelines. The point is to practice writing and hear the Creator's voice. If you and your child finish early, don't feel pressure to extend the exercise. If you don't finish an exercise within the suggested time frame, feel free to keep going or return to it later.

Hearing God's voice: The most important element of this companion guide is the Creator's voice. That is why the first exercise is based on chapter 24 of *Radiance*, where she meets the Creator for the first time. Beyond that point, the exercises follow the book in order.

Reading plan: I've included a generalized reading plan for those who are going through the novel and the companion guide at the same time. You can find it in the following lesson plan. Reading the novel is not required to complete this guide, but it is recommended.

Depth of imagination: Finally, this guide can be used more than once because you're interacting with the Creator, who says different things in different ways. It's possible for multiple stories and "creative experiments" to come out of the same exercise. Pay attention to the lovely things that emerge from these times with Jesus, and help your child see the depth of his or her imaginative experiences with him.

Evaluating your child's work: At the end of this guide, you'll find some simple, basic tips for evaluating your child's work. Writers, like other artistic individuals, can be very sensitive. Anything involving correction and creativity needs to be handled with gentleness, so the child (or adult) doesn't end up closing the door on future creativity.

LESSON PLAN

Please go through this guide in the way that fits your family best. Here's a down-to-earth lesson plan that might work well for you and your children:

Fire Lesson 1

1. Read the included material from Chapter 24: "The Sitting Room in the Woods."
2. Complete the writing exercise.
3. Discuss the completed exercise. How does your child's story reveal Jesus?

Radiance reading plan: Chapters 1-3

Fire Lesson 2

1. Read the included material from Chapter 4: "A Conversation in the Sea."
2. Complete the writing exercise.
3. Discuss the completed exercise. What is Jesus like in your child's story?

Radiance reading plan: Chapters 4-6

Fire Lesson 3

1. Read the included material from Chapter 6: "The Fire Has Shifted."
2. Complete the writing exercise.
3. Discuss the completed exercise. Why is hearing God's voice important?

Radiance reading plan: Chapters 7-10

Fire Lesson 4

1. Read the included material from Chapter 12: "Firestone."
2. Complete the writing exercise.
3. Discuss the completed exercise. How does your child's story reveal Jesus?

Radiance reading plan: Chapters 11-14

Fire Lesson 5

1. Read the included material from Chapter 19: "The Heritage of Water."
2. Complete the writing exercise.
3. Discuss the completed exercise. How has Jesus gifted your child?

Radiance reading plan: Chapters 15-18

Fire Lesson 6

1. Read the included material from Chapter 20: "Hawk Talks About the Wind."
2. Complete the writing exercise.
3. Discuss the completed exercise. How does the Creator speak to your child?

Radiance reading plan: Chapters 19-21

Fire Lesson 7

1. Read the included material from Chapter 22: "The Tree House."
2. Complete the writing exercise.
3. Discuss the completed exercise. What does your child believe about the kindness of God?

Radiance reading plan: Chapter 22

Fire Lesson 8

1. Read the included material from Chapter 22: "The Tree House."
2. Complete the writing exercise.
4. Discuss the completed exercise. How does your child's story reveal Jesus?

Radiance reading plan: Chapters 23-24

Fire Lesson 9

1. Read the included material from Chapter 23: "Radiance Goes to See."
2. Complete the writing exercise.
3. Discuss the completed exercise. What is the Creator currently speaking to your child's heart?

Radiance reading plan: Chapter 25

Fire Lesson 10

1. Read the included material from Chapter 25: "The Door of Stone and Fire."
2. Complete the writing exercise.
3. Discuss the completed exercise. What is your child asking God for?

Radiance reading plan: Chapters 26-27

Fire Lesson 11

1. Read the included material from Chapter 26: "Ruwok's Fire."
2. Complete the writing exercise.
3. Discuss the completed exercise. How does your child's story show who Jesus is?

Radiance reading plan: Chapter 28

Fire Lesson 12

1. Read the included material from Chapter 26: "Ruwok's Fire."
2. Complete the writing exercise.
3. Discuss the completed exercise. Does your child understand how much God loves the sound of his or her voice?

Radiance reading plan: Chapters 29-30

Fire Lesson 13

1. Read the included material from Chapter 27: "The Adventure."
2. Complete the writing exercise.
3. Discuss the completed exercise. Why does God enjoy adventures?

Radiance reading plan: Chapter 31
(Chapter 31 concludes the novel.)

Fire Lesson 14

1. Read the included material from Chapter 30: "Unexpected News."
2. Complete the writing exercise.
3. Discuss the completed exercise. What is your child thankful for?

Fire Lesson 15

1. Read the scene involving Radiance and her father. (This is an extra scene that did not appear in the novel.)
2. Complete the writing exercise.
3. Discuss the completed exercise. How does your child's story reveal Jesus?

Ruwok spoke three words. *"She is fire."*

Somehow just the sound of his voice was a relief. Hawk determined he would explain this to Radiance, possibly early in the morning, when he continued her lessons. Hearing Ruwok's voice was a *relief* that changed what needed to be changed in a person's heart.

"Yes, Edofan," Hawk replied. "She's a flamemaker. Indeed, her presence here in Theraine is quite unexpected. Another of your surprises." Radiance would shock the entire nation when they heard of her. They would respond the way the ambassador had responded this evening—in utter disbelief.

But then Ruwok spoke again, and Hawk grew still.

"No, Hawk." A gentle summer wind, one that stirred flowers and tree leaves and told the earth of abundance, that all was well. *"She is fire."*

FIRE LESSON 1

BASED ON CHAPTER 24
"THE SITTING ROOM IN THE WOODS"

READ

"Flamemakers can feel heat," Radiance said as she picked her way carefully down the mountain. She held her fire-hand high in the air, away from all the leaves and the growing things around her feet. She could put out a fire as easily as she could start one, but tonight she had more important things to do. "People. Bears. Fireplaces. We can feel all those things. And sunlight—we can feel sunlight. *And* we can feel if something has been sitting in the sunlight. Like a rock. There are times when we can even feel rocks."

Leaning up against the trunk of a huge tree, she pulled at the strap of her right sandal and finally worked her foot free. Letting the sandal slide to the ground, she watched where it disappeared in the shadows. "Don't forget where you put your sandals," she told herself sternly before dragging off the other one.

Then she straightened up and put her fists on her hips, cocking her head as her bare feet told her exactly what she thought they would say.

The forest floor was warm. She closed her eyes and pretended she was standing in a fireplace. Not *next* to a fireplace, but actually inside one, where the flames had gone out but the embers still glowed. That was what the forest floor was like.

"You don't make any sense," she told the earth. Why was the ground *warm*—in the middle of the night?

She prowled down the mountainside until the trees parted and she came to a little clearing, where heat poured out of the ground in waves. The air and ground were so hot that her mind said she should see flames. Surely the clearing was on fire, completely engulfed.

But there was nothing. Only quiet and moonlight and black, silent trees.

"This," she whispered to the heat she could feel but couldn't see with her eyes, "is very strange."

As if in answer, light sparked through the trees on the clearing's other side. This time the flash had looked golden, like firelight. *It's changing colors,* she thought and frowned down at the soil under her bare toes. Light that changed colors, and ground that was as hot as fire, yet nothing burned.

Interesting.

Leaving her shoes behind, she crossed the clearing and crept around the trees, climbing over fallen trunks that radiated heat she could feel all over her body. When she touched the slowly rotting wood with her fingertips, it was as if she'd dipped her fingers in boiling soup. Fire and more fire. A significant blaze.

But nothing was there. She nearly laughed. *How odd this is.* She couldn't run back up the mountain now, not with such a mystery waiting for her. Hawk would understand—he liked mysteries too. *I will go and find this fire that doesn't burn.*

Light rushed through branches, pine needles, and fluttering leaves ahead of her, and at last she drew close enough to see what the light was—the source of the heat that spread through the air and pumped through the soil. Hiding behind a tree, she squinted at one of the strangest sights she'd ever seen.

Someone had set up a sitting room in the middle of the woods.

A couch and chair sat facing one another. A white basin filled with fire rested between them where a table or rug would usually go. The fire blazed a host of different shades of yellow and gold, like normal fire, but then—to Radiance's utter surprise—it washed white. Blindingly white, so much so that she winced and lifted her hand to shield her eyes. As she watched, the fire changed again, darkening into a rainbow of reds—many, many types of scarlet and crimson, each color alive with light. Then the fire flashed again, this time almost blue, but not quite. Almost green, but not exactly green either. Radiance's eyes widened as she realized she actually didn't know what this color was. Flames that changed colors. And so *many* colors…

She lifted her head and saw three doors standing on the other side of the fire basin.

There was no wall to hold the doors in place, yet they stood upright as if a wall existed. The first door appeared to be made of heavy steel, like something found at Northpost. The second door looked like it had come off the front of a house. A regular house—someone's home.

The third door was made of molten rock and fire. The inside of it burned, gleaming red through cracks and creases in the black rock.

That one. That was the one she would open first.

She slid out from behind her tree and ventured a few steps into the sitting room. Was this usual in Theraine, to find a fiery sitting room in the middle of the woods? Invisible fire burned in the air. She could feel it filling her lungs every time she took a breath. No Theranian would ever step foot here—not even Hawk. This was a flamemaker's sitting room. A perfect place.

The fire door tugged at her the way water did. It was like she could *feel* the door somehow, even from several steps away. She slid one step closer—and that was when the man on the couch stood up. For the first time she saw him. She froze, shoulders bunched, all her muscles tight.

He looked to be about thirty years old. His hair was as white as the fire now burning in the basin. It almost seemed to be the same as the fire, which didn't make any sense at all. And his eyes—

His eyes.

She stared at him.

"Hello, Radiance," he said. A voice like fire, like every fire she had ever heard crackling and burning but more so, all at once. "We've been waiting for you in Theraine."

The prophet's words, a distant voice in her head recognized. She could barely move. "Who are you, sir?" she whispered, the words lost in all the fire. More than she loved fire, more than she loved water, she suddenly had to know.

"Someone who has waited a long time to be a main character in your story," he replied kindly.

And from that point forward, no one needed to explain anything else. She had no questions about who this man was. She looked into his fire eyes—the eyes of a deep blaze—and just knew.

Ruwok.

WRITING *EXERCISE*

Imagine yourself in Ruwok's sitting room out in the woods. Everywhere you look there is fire, and it's like you can feel his fire in your bones.

Describe the scene: what the air smells like, what the heat feels like, if there's any wind, if there's something interesting about the furniture, etc. What does Ruwok (picture Jesus) say to you? What is it like to speak with him? Does he send you on an adventure?

Time: Write as much as you can for 15 minutes.

LAUREN STINTON

BASED ON CHAPTER 4
"A CONVERSATION IN THE SEA"

READ

"How do you know my name?" Radiance asked.

The man just looked at her. Then he walked into the waves and sat down right beside her, so close she could have touched him. Water coursed over his trousers. In just seconds he appeared to be completely soaked from the waist down.

Radiance blinked in surprise. She could not imagine Mr. Liam sitting down in the water with her, but this man didn't seem to mind having the sea in all his clothes. He actually let out a little sigh like he'd been waiting to sit down all day.

"I heard your teacher say it," he explained at last. "He spoke it quite forcefully, in fact. My name is Hawk."

"Like the bird?" she asked.

There was a smile in his voice as he replied, "Yes. Like the bird." He paused. "I know that I offended you today when you asked if I was a flamemaker. I don't know *how* I offended you, but I'm sorry I did. There are times when I say the wrong thing, and I'm not sure how it happens, because much of the time I know good words and how they should be said."

Radiance glanced at him again. He was staring out across the sea, and she decided to forgive him because he looked at the water the same way she did. Also he was sitting in the sea with her, and she couldn't very well be upset with a man who was willing to sit in the sea with her.

"What are you?" she asked. "Your gift, I mean."

His beard moved, and this time she saw his smile clearly in the moonlight. "My name doesn't give it away?"

"Your name?"

"I am a hawk. A bird that loves the wind."

Only one gift would find the wind so interesting. She sighed. "Oh…you're a weathermaker?"

He laughed. "You don't have to sound *that* disappointed."

She stared at him and then—several seconds later—started laughing too. Maybe it was the saltwater, but she felt so very relaxed here, like a real person. He turned and grinned at her. The moonlight reflecting in his eyes told her he was pleased with her response, and she decided to forgive him every time he said the wrong thing, not just this time.

"I talked to the innkeeper today, and he told me about your school." Hawk's voice changed. "I'm sorry about your parents, Radiance. Sincerely. It is very sad to grow up alone."

There was something in his voice that made her want to study him closely. He sounded like he *knew*. Like he wasn't only being sympathetic. He was looking out to sea again, and she thought—it was just a sense—that he might be able to understand her more than anyone else could. She eased toward him. "Are your parents dead too?"

He hesitated before shaking his head. "No, but I have not seen them in a long time. Since long before you were born."

"Why? Did something happen? Did you fight?" She knew that happened with adults sometimes. They fought about things, and sometimes they were sorry about it later.

He leaned back, putting his weight on his hands buried in the watery sand behind him. "That's a long story. Perhaps I will tell it to you sometime." He frowned. "Look, Radiance. How long have you been at the Marble Town School for Girls?"

"A long time."

"How long is *a long time*?"

"Years and years. I can't remember living any other place. Where were you born? You have an accent."

His head slowly turned, and he gave her his full attention. His eyes narrowed, and his head tipped to the side like he needed to examine her from a different angle.

When he spoke next, she took a quick breath because she didn't know any of the words. The language seemed to flow with the sea. It rose up and down like waves and somehow seemed salty and windy both at once. Because it reminded her of the sea, she instantly loved it.

"Is that the language they speak where you were born?" she asked.

WRITING *EXERCISE*

In this part of Radiance's story, she and Hawk sit in the sea together and have a conversation. Imagine you're a flamemaker who loves the sea the way Radiance does. What would it be like to walk along the beach at night? To get your feet wet in the water? What would the breeze smell like, and how would the moon reflect on the waves?

Now imagine Jesus is walking next to you. Write a story about what happens.

Time: Write for 15 minutes.

BASED ON CHAPTER 6
"THE FIRE HAS SHIFTED"

READ

"You are about to go on an adventure. Yes, it's unexpected. Yes, it might be a little bit scary. But are you ready?"

Yes. She was ready.

She was a *flamemaker*. Fire burned in her blood, and she would always want the adventure. She had to have the freedom to move—to go places and touch things and do what her gift wanted to do. The fire was a part of her. It was exactly what she was like.

Maybe this man understood. He was Theranian, and they didn't have any flamemakers over there, but there was a strange light in his eyes that made her think he knew something she did not. Something important. And he'd said he would show her the sea.

"What do you think?" he asked and smiled like he already knew her answer.

"I would like to be shown the sea, sir," she said.

His smile widened. "Yes, I thought you might."

WRITING *EXERCISE*

Write a story about a flamemaker who has to take a message to someone living on a mountain. As a flamemaker, your main character can create fire. She (or he) isn't burned by fire, and she never feels cold.

Your main character can also hear Ruwok's voice. Maybe she can hear it the same way Radiance does (he sounds like fire), or maybe she hears it some other way. Be creative.

Try to answer the following questions in your story:

1. Why is the message important?
2. Who or what tries to keep your main character from reaching her destination?
3. How does Ruwok help your main character?

Time: Write as much as you can for 15 minutes.

THE FIRE WRITER

FIRE LESSON 4

BASED ON CHAPTER 12
"FIRESTONE"

READ

For two days, they traveled along the coastline, sleeping each night next to the sea. The second night they were close enough to a little village that they could see the lights through the trees. Basir, apparently, had no desire to be near landers because he picked a spot for their small camp on the sand next to a rock. They ate fish that Kian caught with a spear, and they talked about things that weren't important. After days of language lessons and Theranian history, Radiance thought it was pleasant to talk about unimportant things. What she had learned about in school. If she liked warm water more than cold water, or if it didn't matter because of her fire.

On the third night, the sky opened up and a storm rolled in over the sea.

Radiance stood on the beach with her arms out and her head back as the wind and rain lashed the sand. The moment was perfect—she almost felt cold.

Hawk stepped up next to her. He wasn't wearing a coat either. *Weathermaker*, she thought with a smile. Perhaps there was some benefit to that gift after all.

"Can you do it here as well?" he asked over the storm. "In the rain?"

He didn't have to explain. She knew exactly what he meant.

She brought her hand up in front of her, and fire bloomed from her palm, casting orangey light on her clothes and arms and making the raindrops seem to spark. These were flames that mocked the night and all the rain.

"I've tried this before," she said. "Using my gift in the rain."

"What about lakes? Bath water? Sinks? Water closets? Did you try all those places too?"

She nodded. "Of course."

He laughed, rain rolling down his face. "Of course. My gift is the same way. It does odd things at times but only in saltwater. You will find that saltwater is special. Any water is good, but saltwater—that's really where you want to be, Ray."

The glow inside her grew a little brighter at his use of her special name. "Because we came from there?"

Thunder rumbled. The sea slammed into the sand over and over, and as she stared out across the water, she briefly forgot she'd asked a question. She wanted to be out there—in a little boat where every single wave washed over the side and soaked her clean through.

"Yes," Hawk said. "That's why."

He lifted his hand above his head and spread out his fingers. Rain pounded against his open palm. The next time lightning flared through the sky, white-blue light spiraled toward the beach, cutting through the darkness until the last slash of light struck Hawk's hand with full force.

Wind blasted Radiance's wet hair from her shoulders. She staggered back to keep her balance, tingles racing back and forth across her skin. As she saw the utter joy on Hawk's face, she started laughing and couldn't stop.

Water dripped off his beard and ran down all sides of his bald scalp. He had just caught a bolt of lightning in his hand, and for a moment it was like the current still flickered in his eyes.

"What?" he asked, smiling like a little boy. Radiance didn't know many little boys, but she could imagine they looked just like this when they were happy. "Didn't you know a weathermaker could do that?"

"What else can a weathermaker do?" she asked, because she didn't wish to go back to their camp and—so it seemed—neither did he.

She and Hawk. They were made for storms. For harsh nights just like this one.

WRITING *EXERCISE*

What would it be like to catch lightning with your hand?

Imagine you're standing on a beach with Jesus. A fierce storm rages all around you, but you aren't afraid. What does it feel like to be next to Jesus in the middle of a storm? What does he say to you, and what do the two of you do together as the wind blows and the rain beats down on the beach?

Time: Write as much as you can in 15 minutes.

THE FIRE WRITER

BASED ON CHAPTER 19
"THE HERITAGE OF WATER"

READ

"This," Hawk said, "is called *shifting*. Just as water can shift from a solid form to a vaporous form, so can we. This is one of the distinct differences between soil and water—between us and our lander counterparts. Another difference is how we age, of course. But we can talk about that some other time."

Radiance barely heard any of this. "What…are you doing to me?"

"I told you. I shifted you."

She could hear the smile in his voice, but she could no longer see him. He stood in front of her—and she couldn't see him.

No, wait. That wasn't true. She *could* see him, but it was like staring at a person standing in shadows. She could see the outline of his body but none of his details, like his eyes or his nose or his expression.

With her free hand, Radiance reached forward slowly and tried to push her finger against Hawk's shoulder. She knew he was wearing a blue tunic today, but she couldn't see it, and now she couldn't even feel it. It was as if he had turned into mist. A body crafted out of mist. Her finger couldn't find him, though he stood right in front of her.

"What *is* this?" she breathed, pulling her finger back.

"Do you like it?"

"I love it. I love it wildly."

He chuckled. "Your Theranian parent would have taught you all about these things. So I will teach you instead."

"I can't touch your shoulder."

"Not in this form, no."

"But you're still holding my hand. I can't see it, but I can feel it."

The misty shape of his head nodded. "Water can do many things, Radiance. It can be a solid. It can be a liquid. It can be a vapor. With experience, you'll be able to control the *amount* you shift. This ability to change form is incredibly helpful on the battlefield, when your enemies can see you but can't hurt you because of the form you've taken."

He shrugged. She felt the slight pull of his hand and saw the ghostly movement of his shoulders. "Fire, of course, makes things a bit more difficult. That's part of the reason many of us feel a little anxious around flamemakers. In my shifted state, no one could shoot me with an arrow or use a sword against me—it would pass through me harmlessly. But *you* could use your gift and injure me. Fire forces us to shift back into a solid form. It can hurt us when nothing can hurt us, if that makes sense, which is why we're afraid of it."

"Is this why Theranians don't like to be touched—because sometimes they *can't* be touched and people fall right through them?"

He laughed again but gently. "Not quite, though that's a logical conclusion. Many years ago when our ancestors first settled in Theraine, they used lawmakers to hide our true identity from the landers. It was thought this would help us finally have peace with our neighbors. If our neighbors didn't know what we were, they wouldn't have any reason to be afraid of us. So we hid ourselves."

As Radiance wiggled her invisible fingers in front of her face, she remembered what Basir had told her about the history of her new nation. They couldn't live with the full-blooded e'nethaine in the sea, and they couldn't live with full-blooded landers outside the sea. No one wanted them, and so they'd made their own country.

"It was written," Hawk went on, "that our nation would be hidden from landers until Ruwok gave someone the special ability to *unravel* the law. That hasn't happened yet, but one day—soon, it is thought—that person will do what Ruwok said."

Letting go of Radiance's hand, Hawk shifted back into his regular form. He *appeared* there in front of her, becoming solid again.

Radiance stared at him. *This is wondrous.*

"If you were listening to our conversation yesterday," he said, "Jesse spoke of the lawmakers. Someday what has been hidden will be revealed. But *until* that time, we avoid the healers of other nations. The secret of the sea in our blood is protected from every gift, but a healer will always know what we are, because of the nature of their gift."

He shook his head. "Any healer who touched you would know you're part e'nethaine. That you're a water dweller." His brows lifted in a way that reminded her of Basir. "That's why it was interesting to learn a healer had brought you to the school in Marble Town. The moment he touched you, he would have known what you were—but did he shout and proclaim what he'd discovered? No. He was quiet about it. One day I'd like to find out why. A discovery of an e'nethaine child would have made him famous in King's Barrow, where every sighting of e'nethaine is carefully recorded and preserved. Everyone would have rushed to Marble Town to see you, and your life would have been very different. With his decision to say nothing, he helped keep you safe."

"Water and fire," she said and thrust her hand into the air, spurting flame off the tip of her finger. But only a small flame, something that wouldn't make her friend Hawk nervous.

Hawk grinned. "That's exactly what you are. Water and fire. A marvelous combination."

WRITING **EXERCISE**

The Creator made you in a unique way so you can know him yourself and do good things that help people. Just as Radiance has a special purpose and calling, so do you.

Imagine yourself sitting beside Jesus on the edge of a cliff that overlooks the sea. Describe the scene. Is it nighttime or daytime? What do you see around you? What does the breeze feel like? Ask Jesus how he's gifted you, and write what he says.

Time: Write as much as you can for 15 minutes.

FIRE LESSON 6

BASED ON CHAPTER 20

"HAWK TALKS ABOUT THE WIND"

READ

Talking about her parents this way made Radiance feel a little sad. Her parents must have loved each other very much—they *must* have, because one was water and the other was fire. An unlikely match. Even Hawk sometimes seemed a bit nervous around her fire, and he was her friend. But her Theranian parent had somehow overcome this fear to fall in love with a flamemaker, only to die a few years later when Radiance was just a baby.

She sighed. *Such a sad story.* Only readers liked sad stories—she had learned this from Mrs. Semos, who said she liked to cry when she read books—but Radiance's fire did not like to cry. She wanted happy stories, things that turned out well and stayed well.

Taking a breath, she asked to keep the sadness away, "Did Ruwok *really* tell you that Cale and I would be at the king's storehouse?"

"Yes."

"But how? How did he say it?" An idea jumped into her head—a memory of something she'd heard at her old school. "Does he sound like thunder? I've heard that weathermakers can talk to one another with thunder. It's like another language, but one only your clan can speak."

Hawk shrugged, his shoulders lifting and falling in front of her nose. "When I hear him, he doesn't sound much like thunder."

"But weathermakers *can* speak to each other with thunder, can't they?"

"Of course. But thunder is *loud*. It's something anybody can hear. Conversations with thunder are unmistakable. Every weathermaker within several miles can tell what's being said—it's like someone shouting from one rooftop to another. There's no secrecy."

He turned slightly in the saddle so he could see her a little better. "Ruwok made the gifts, and he picked who would receive each of the gifts he made. He crafted bloodlines and families and planned how his gifts would flow through them the way rivers flow across a continent. It only makes sense that he would continue his interest in people throughout their lifetimes. This is important to understand because Ruwok speaks to people *according* to their gifts."

"So, because you're a weathermaker—" she began.

He was already nodding. "Yes. Because I am a weathermaker, when he speaks to me, he sounds like an element of my gift. For me, he sounds like the wind. I don't hear his voice the way I hear thunder. Most of the time it isn't loud and booming, but it's like a quiet wind inside me. I was named for the wind, so it makes sense that he would speak to me with something I understand. I went to the king's storehouse because that is what Ruwok told me to do. I've learned he will speak to me especially when I am listening."

He turned back around, leaving Radiance to think about these things.

WRITING *EXERCISE*

When the Creator speaks to Radiance, he sounds like fire. When he speaks to Hawk, he sounds like a quiet wind. Both of them can hear his voice even when they can't see him with their eyes.

The Creator can speak in many different ways: through what you hear with your ears or with your spirit, what you sense (a feeling inside you), what you remember, what you find yourself thinking about, or sometimes even what you smell. His voice often sounds like a thought or an idea that comes to you, and he also loves to speak in pictures in your imagination.

How does the Creator speak to you? Ask him to tell you what he thinks about you, and write his words below. If he shows you a picture, describe it as best you can with words.

Time: Try to write for 15 minutes.

THE FIRE WRITER

FIRE LESSON 7

BASED ON CHAPTER 22
"THE TREE HOUSE"

READ

When Hawk did not quickly return, Radiance began to practice her shifting. She had practiced many times on the road today, and she thought she was getting better at it. Turning herself invisible didn't feel nearly as strange as it had at the beginning.

First she shifted her finger, the one inserted in the fountain's steady stream. Her skin and all her bones disappeared as she watched, and then she made the invisibleness creep up the rest of her hand, then her wrist, then slowly up her arm. It felt a little like tightening and relaxing her muscles. It wasn't hard to do, but it did take practice.

She had almost reached her elbow when a voice said right at her ear, "You're right, of course. You are much better at this now."

She shouted and jerked back into someone's body. Hands clamped around her arms to keep her from falling, and the man started laughing.

"Ho!" he said. "I shall remember this for the future—do not surprise young flamemakers when they're concentrating."

The hands quickly released her as she whirled around, and of all the people it could have been—Hawk, the ambassador, the servants who had eventually appeared—it was the prophet who stood behind her. He beamed with apparent pleasure even as he shook his hands wildly, trying to put out an invisible fire.

"The fire of surprise," he said. "Still just as hot! I'm glad you're practicing the natural abilities Ruwok has assigned to your people, young lady. This is good, and it will benefit you."

Your people. Not *our people.* Wasn't he Theranian? She thought he was Theranian. But maybe he wasn't, and maybe that's why he stood so close to her now. He didn't back up and give her plenty of space the way Basir would, especially if she'd nearly burned his hands.

The prophet narrowed his eyes and made a show of peering down at her. Though he was close to Hawk's age, he managed to squish his face until there were so many wrinkles that she could barely see what he looked like on the other side of them, and she found herself grinning even as her heart ran nearly as fast as it could. The prophet had come to talk to her.

"You know," he said, tapping the side of his nose, "I see many things when I look at you. Things in your future and things in your past."

The pounding in her chest reached out into her entire body.

"And if I were to give you a prophecy—a few words that might help you right now—I think this would be the most important thing I could say." The wrinkles eased, and with light in his eyes, the prophet said gently, "Ruwok is kind. That is a perfect word, and the plan he has for you will make you laugh. There. That was not a scary prophecy, was it?" He winked at her.

"No, sir," she replied, somewhat surprised. "It wasn't scary at all."

"Good. For I dearly hate frightening children." He winced. "That is to say, I do not like frightening *them*. They don't actually frighten *me*. I don't find children scary. Do you find them scary?"

She laughed and decided she liked him. What a strange thing—to like a prophet. "Do you always give people prophecies, sir?"

"Often, yes."

"Have you ever given a prophecy to a flamemaker before?"

"Oh yes, several times. But a Theranian flamemaker? A child capable of mixing fire and water—of knowing Ruwok in two very different ways?" His brows lifted. "This is the first time."

WRITING *EXERCISE*

The Prophet of Theraine tells Radiance that Ruwok is kind. How is Ruwok kind to Radiance in her story?

Do you think Jesus is kind? This is one way the Bible talks about his heart:

> *The Lord's lovingkindnesses indeed never cease,*
> *For His compassions never fail.*
> *They are new every morning;*
> *Great is Your faithfulness. (Lam. 3:22-23)*

What do you think that passage means? Write about it in your own words.

Time: Write for 15 minutes.

THE FIRE WRITER

FIRE LESSON 8

BASED ON CHAPTER 22
"THE TREE HOUSE"

READ

"But the prophet *also* told me something I think you will like." He suddenly smiled at her. "I am fairly certain you will like this, in fact. I like it myself—it just was not what I expected."

She leaned forward eagerly. "What is it? What did he say?"

The smile remained in his eyes as he replied, "He told me there was a reason *I* found you in King's Barrow, that it was me and no one else. You and I are going to be together for a very long time, Radiance. I thought I would be with Basir for a long time, but the prophet tells me that it's you." His voice softened. "You are the reason I became a tefilah. Everything I was doing for Basir—I am now going to do these things for you instead."

He hesitated. "But I don't know why. To speak honestly, you are yet a child and many things are unknown about you. Very few children in Theraine are assigned tefilah. Yet there is something about you that Ruwok wishes to keep closely protected. So here I am. To do his will."

WRITING *EXERCISE*

*He makes the winds His messengers,
Flaming fire His ministers.
(Ps.104:4)*

Using Psalm 104:4 as your base, write something that expresses your heart. It could be a story, a conversation with God, your ideas about what this verse means, etc. The point is to take this verse and be *creative* in the presence of the Lord.

If you read the verse and nothing comes to mind, here are a few ideas to help you get started. Try to be as creative as possible.

1. In Radiance's world, how could the wind deliver a message from the Creator?
2. If you were a weathermaker like Hawk, how could you use the wind to help you?
3. What do you think Radiance would say about this verse because she loves fire so much?
4. What do you think it means for fire to "minister" to God?

Time: Write for at least 15 minutes.

FIRE LESSON 9

BASED ON CHAPTER 23
"RADIANCE GOES TO SEE"

READ

Hawk waited until Radiance was asleep.

Then he eased off his bedroll and slipped out from under the drooping tree branches and into the wilds of the night. As he sneaked away, he thought it likely that this would be a regular occurrence with them—one of them sleeping, the other one sneaking. Back and forth. Why? Because they were similar. Both of them liked to sneak off in the nighttime to go do interesting things.

But tonight Hawk had a purpose he couldn't overlook. Something he had to do.

Pausing beside his horse, he rubbed the animal's nose in silent greeting and then turned north, climbing up the mountain slope until the pine tree where Radiance slept was just one shadow of many far below him. In the patchy blacks and grays of the woods, with mere splinters of moonlight bearing down on him, he found a rather flat section of earth and lay on his stomach, arms stretched out to either side.

That was how he spoke to the Creator.

Not every tefilah spoke to Ruwok this way. Some preferred to walk or pace, to sit in a chair, to write in a journal. But Hawk felt like he and Ruwok had an understanding—one that looked like *this*, with his face to the ground.

"You surprised me today, Edofan," he began, using an ancient title for the

Creator of the world. "Surprise seems to be the…the song of your heart lately." He released the air from his lungs and said against the soil, "I don't know what you're doing. Radiance is special to me, as you well know, and I do not regret your decision in the slightest. Staying with her? That will be a joy. But I do wish I knew what you were doing."

He spoke like this for quite some time until, all at once, the answer came quietly. A wind deep inside him. Words that moved and turned, barely staying still for longer than a moment. Here and then gone, leaving weight and knowing behind. He knew this voice—this internal breeze that would always be dear to him.

Ruwok spoke three words. *"She is fire."*

Somehow just the sound of his voice was a relief. Hawk determined he would explain this to Radiance, possibly early in the morning, when he continued her lessons. Hearing Ruwok's voice was a *relief* that changed what needed to be changed in a person's heart.

"Yes, Edofan," Hawk replied. "She's a flamemaker. Indeed, her presence here in Theraine is quite unexpected. Another of your surprises." Radiance would shock the entire nation when they heard of her. They would respond the way the ambassador had responded this evening—in utter disbelief.

But then Ruwok spoke again, and Hawk grew still.

"No, Hawk." A gentle summer wind, one that stirred flowers and tree leaves and told the earth of abundance, that all was well. *"She is fire."*

WRITING *EXERCISE*

In this part of Radiance's story, Hawk feels uneasy. Something is bothering him, and he knows what he needs—he needs to go talk to Ruwok.

Think of something that's bothering you. It could be anything: an argument with a loved one, a scary dream, a worry, or something one of your friends said. Ask the Lord to help you with it. Write your prayer below.

Afterward imagine that you're talking to Jesus out in the woods. Trees stand tall all around you, and the silvery moon hangs high above your head. Ask the Lord what he wants to tell you about this thing that bothers you, and write down what you think he says.

Time: Write for 15 minutes.

THE FIRE WRITER

FIRE LESSON 10

BASED ON CHAPTER 25
"THE DOOR OF STONE AND FIRE"

READ

Radiance stared, unmoving, as Ruwok reached into his pocket and pulled out a gold watch. It seemed to be made of its own kind of fire. It grew brighter as he flipped it open and looked down at the time. Then he glanced at her, brows rising. A smile twitched his lips.

"Do you know what this is?" he asked and held the watch so she could see it clearly.

She did—it was a watch. She nodded slowly, not daring to speak and wondering if maybe a watch could be something *other* than a watch. This was Ruwok. Surely he knew what a watch was.

"Everything I do," Ruwok said, "I do with precision. If I ask someone to wait, it is always for a reason." He shook the watch, drawing her attention back to it. "And for a specific time. I have asked you to wait for something, Radiance. But now the time has come for me to give you what you have been waiting for."

His smile widened, and Radiance couldn't look away. Never in her life had she seen a face so free of fear. He was surrounded by fire. It filled the air, but Ruwok appeared perfectly at ease. This was *his* sitting room, she realized. It was like he was a flamemaker, just as she was.

God of fire.

She gasped. It was true, wasn't it? That was what he was. Why had no one ever spoken those words to her? She should have known this about Ruwok years and years ago. How comforting those words would have been to her heart—that he wasn't afraid of her gift like everyone else was. He wasn't afraid even a little bit. Ruwok understood her, didn't he? More than Hawk. More than anyone, because he was fire too.

He turned and gestured with the watch toward the three doors standing nearby. One door made of steel. One door from a house. One door made of stone and fire.

"I," he announced in a voice that sounded close to laughter, "am telling three key stories in the earth right now. Would you like to see what they are?"

She nodded, mute. She thought she would always say yes to him, especially now. *Fire.*

WRITING *EXERCISE*

Sometimes the Creator asks us to wait for what we want. Have you ever had to wait for something? Maybe you've prayed about something important, and you're still waiting for God to answer that prayer. Or maybe there's something you really want to do with your life, but it will take a while.

Write your prayer request. Then ask God what he thinks about it, and write down his answer. If he gives you a picture (something you can see in your imagination), describe the picture the way you would write a story.

Time: Write as much as you can for 15 minutes.

FIRE LESSON 11

BASED ON CHAPTER 26
"RUWOK'S FIRE"

READ

All around Radiance, the night sky filled with the light of dawn—a sun drawing closer and closer. This was not a sun taking a slow and steady walk through the sky, like a sun normally would, but this sun sprinted. All the other stars seemed to fade as the star Ruwok had called swept closer.

A new and different kind of fire began to wash across Radiance's skin. Her gift seemed to shiver as if surprised, and then it began to laugh. That was the only description that came to mind as Ruwok's star approached. Radiance gripped his hand and laughed and laughed and thought about dancing.

Heat rippled through the air. It was good, she thought, that she wasn't in the woods anymore because all the trees would have burst into flames, and all the rocks would have caught fire, and all the Theranians would have hated it. Radiance, however, thrust her hand up into the air and watched as the vivid light and brilliant heat ran across her fingertips in fiery waves. Purple, gold, blue, white. All of it was lovely.

When it seemed like nothing existed in the entire world but fire and burning, Radiance became aware of a person standing in front of her—a *shifted* person, or so it seemed, because she could see only the woman's fluid outline.

"Hello," Ruwok greeted and then said the star's name. Again the long line of sounds spilled out of his mouth. Sounds Radiance would never be able to say or recognize. The only part she managed to grasp was the last sound. It seemed much like *Ella*, a girl's name.

That's her, Radiance thought. The star was called Ella.

"Edofan," the star said in a voice that rippled and tore and blazed like the heart of fire.

Radiance stared and wished she could see the woman more clearly. *A star. This is a star.*

"This is the young flamemaker I told you about," Ruwok said simply and held up his hand, the one wrapped around Radiance's.

Radiance felt the star's eyes. They were prophet's eyes—the same kind of pressure that felt almost like hands on her face. Last year in school, Radiance and the other girls had studied the stars and what ancient readers said about them. One historian wrote that the stars could see the future. Radiance hadn't remembered that description until now, when all at once she understood what it meant and why it meant that. Stars were prophets. That was how Ruwok had made them.

The wavering outline bent in two, and Radiance realized the woman had knelt down. She gasped as she found herself eye to eye with a star. A flamemaker of another sort.

"Hello, Radiance," the fire-voice said gently. It was a thousand fires contained in a single throat. She spoke with an accent that made Radiance start thinking about star charts and faraway places—places so distant they didn't even know about the earth. "I have something that belongs to you. It was entrusted to me many years ago—years as your earth would count them, when the whole of creation was only a few days old. Ruwok says it is now time for you to have this gift."

WRITING *EXERCISE*

*I am the one who made the earth and created people to live on it. With my hands I stretched out the heavens.
All the stars are at my command.*
(Isa. 45:12 NLT)

Imagine you are meeting one of the Creator's stars. Describe in detail what it's like and what the two of you talk about. Where is the Creator, and what is he doing? Try to paint a picture for your readers so they feel like they are a part of the story you're telling.

Time: Write for 15 minutes.

BASED ON CHAPTER 26
"RUWOK'S FIRE"

READ

When they had returned to his sitting room, just the two of them, Ruwok knelt down in front of Radiance and smiled.

"Do you know what it means for me to be a main character in your story?" he asked.

She held up one finger. Fire sputtered off the tip. He was a flamemaker too.

He laughed, and the fire that lived and breathed in the air grew even hotter. The fire liked his laughter. "Yes, Radiance. More than you know."

He, too, held up one finger. Fire leapt eagerly off his fingertip, and he touched his fire to hers. "Fire is drawn to fire. This means you will be able to find me when you turn and look for me. Come and find me when you're frightened. Come when you're angry or lonely or confused. My fire will always welcome yours, wherever you are."

She smiled back at him. "I like your voice."

His shoulders lowered as if with a deep sigh, and the fire of his eyes seemed almost to change colors. "I like your voice too."

WRITING *EXERCISE*

Ruwok loves the sound of Radiance's voice. Do you think Jesus loves the sound of your voice? Why or why not?

Picture yourself in a heavenly room, with Jesus sitting beside you. Describe the room in detail. Is it a "normal" room with walls, a floor, and a ceiling? Or is the room unique and completely unexpected? What objects and colors do you see? Is the room full of water, fire, stars, wind, or something else? What does the air smell like? What do you feel inside this room? Use your imagination!

In that room, ask Jesus how he feels about your voice and write his response.

Time: Write for 15 minutes.

THE FIRE WRITER

FIRE LESSON 13

BASED ON CHAPTER 27
"THE ADVENTURE"

READ

Radiance stopped.

She stared out across a vast black field.

All the trees were fire-eaten stumps jutting up into the sky. The rocks looked like mounds of ashes, and everything was dead. The death began a step beyond her bare toes. There was life directly underneath her, where she stood, but there was death everywhere in front of her. She could feel heat slowly drifting out of the blackened earth, but even the heat felt strange—sort of sleepy and stale.

Radiance turned and looked behind her. The trees were green. Birds sang. The sun seemed bright and brilliant.

But in front of her, beyond the "line" in the earth, there was nothing but ashes. No birds. No wind. It seemed that everything had burned up in a fire—but not exactly. Radiance knew what fires were like when they escaped. Last year she'd let a fire escape on purpose, just to see what would happen because she knew the teachers were watching out the window. The flames had jumped from the dead tree to race across the ground. Mr. Liam had panicked, shouting for all the other teachers to come and help him put it out. Just like Radiance suspected, he completely forgot that she was a flamemaker. There wasn't anything for anybody to worry about. All she had to do was put her hand in just one of the flames, and the entire fire rolled away, vanishing into the air. She put the fire out as quickly as she'd started it, as all the teachers shouted at one another then turned and began shouting at her.

Fire liked to do things and go places. The other gifts always had trouble controlling it, so it made them nervous.

Was this a fire that had escaped? But why did it feel so odd to her? There was no smell of smoke in the air. The ashes lay in clumps on the ground, forming unnatural patterns.

Something was strange.

Creeping forward, she squatted down at the line and reached out her hand, first finger extended. She dipped her finger in the ashes and then drew her hand close to her face for inspection. Tiny black bits clung to her skin. She rubbed her finger and thumb together and started frowning. *Like* ashes, but not ashes. Her skin began to tingle wherever the ashes stuck to her. Was it trying to *burn* her?

"This wasn't fire," she told Ruwok and wrinkled her nose.

"No," he replied. *"This was a bad thing that I didn't wish to be done. Yet it was done anyway."*

She thought about all the things he'd told her and what she'd seen—from last night in his sitting room, to the fire-gift from Ella the star, to just now when he'd talked about timing and her feet. "Is this one of those things where you know what to do, but no one else knows?"

His voice warmed. *"Yes. This is the adventure, Radiance—doing what I am doing and going where I am going. This would be a good time to practice your gift. All the things you and I have been talking about. Be wild. Let all your fire come out. Don't hold back."*

She looked out across the burned-up ground that seemed to go on for miles and miles. A long distance away, the earth dipped down around the mountain, and she couldn't tell where the blackness stopped. "Here?"

He seemed to nod. She could almost see it in her mind's eye.

"Yes. Right here."

She smiled slowly. "Truly? *All* my fire?"

"All your fire."

WRITING *EXERCISE*

In this part of Radiance's story, the enemy planned to do something bad, but Ruwok planned to do something *good*. Sometimes bad things happen, but we don't need to be afraid because Jesus has a good plan. He knows exactly what to do.

> *And we know that God causes all things to work together for good to those who love God, to those who are called according to His purpose. (Rom. 8:28)*

Picture yourself standing on a mountain with Jesus. Describe the scene in detail: what you see, hear, feel, think, and smell. What does Jesus tell you, and how does he keep you safe from danger?

Time: Write for 15 minutes.

THE FIRE WRITER

FIRE LESSON 14

BASED ON CHAPTER 30 "UNEXPECTED NEWS"

READ

Hawk held up his hand. "I would issue a warning first, my lord."

Radiance braced herself. Hawk had told her he would do this, but she didn't want to wait. She just wanted all of this to be over. Traveling the road with Hawk and doing exciting things—that was much better than standing here and waiting while a healer looked at her in funny ways and then told her about a family who didn't have any flamemakers. Except for one.

Lord H'lane's head tilted. "A warning, Tefilah? What sort of warning?"

Hawk gestured toward Radiance. "Ruwok recently gave her a *par'salthane*. I, of course, have not seen it myself, but I've been told by another healer that it looks like starlight in her bones. It's a very *unexpected* sight if one is not prepared for it."

Lord H'lane didn't move for a moment. "This child has a *par'salthane*? Which one?"

"The one given for a time of war."

The healer's eyes widened. "The one that rebukes Ruwok's enemies and keeps them at a distance? The one that grows with time until none of his enemies are able to set foot on his land?"

Hawk nodded. "That is the one. We have already seen it at work."

"Now there's a story I would like to know! Yes. Well." Lord H'lane turned back to Radiance. "Aren't you an interesting child, my dear? No wonder the prophet had specific instructions about where you were to go and whom you were to see! Come here, child, and give me your hand. It would seem—or so suggests the prophet—that I know exactly who you are. So let's *see* who you are, shall we?"

At Hawk's encouraging nod, Radiance left the glass fountain behind and walked stiffly across the floor. Lord H'lane held out his hand, and she set hers in his. His long fingers closed over her much shorter ones, and he squinted his eyes as he looked at her.

Nothing happened.

Then she jumped as he dropped her hand.

He stared at her in surprise, and a little voice in her head—not Ruwok's voice, but something very, very different—began telling her what a bad idea this was. She and Hawk never should have come here. This man already didn't like her! And she hadn't even done anything yet.

But then Ruwok's voice appeared in the middle of her thoughts, stopping all of them. She held her breath as he spoke to her. *"Wait. Give it a moment, Radiance. I did not bring you here to injure you. I brought you here to give you a gift."*

A gift? She liked gifts.

"Oh, sweet child," the healer said.

She looked at him in confusion.

He reached forward and wrapped his arms around her and nearly lifted her off her feet. Never mind that she was a stranger to him—and a flamemaker! Never mind that she squeaked a little bit when his arms tightened. "Oh, child!" He said a hundred different things all at once, most of them nothing but unintelligible noises.

She looked over his shoulder at Hawk, who stared at her with equal surprise. He shrugged broadly, both hands level with his ears.

"I don't know," he mouthed to her.

"*This*," Lord H'lane said, "is why Ruwok sent you here. I know why he sent you here!" He pulled away but kept his hands on her arms, gripping her tightly as if he feared she would vanish. And then he said words Radiance had not expected. She had wondered many things about her family, but *this* she had not expected at all.

"I know your father," the healer said, looking into her face earnestly. "He is my good friend, and he is here. He's been here for nine hours! We traveled together from Barantha this morning. *He's here*. He's here."

WRITING *EXERCISE*

The Bible says the Creator gives *good gifts*. Good ones, not bad ones.

> *Every good thing given and every perfect gift is from above, coming down from the Father of lights, with whom there is no variation or shifting shadow.*
> (Jas. 1:17)
>
> *The thief comes only to steal and kill and destroy; I came that they may have life, and have it abundantly.*
> (John 10:10)

Choose one thing you're thankful for, and take it to Jesus. Where do you go to meet with him? Describe the place. Tell him about this thing you're thankful for, and write down what he says. Pay attention to anything he says that surprises you.

Time: Try to write for 15 minutes.

THE FIRE WRITER

FIRE LESSON 15

THIS IS AN EXTRA SCENE NOT INCLUDED IN THE NOVEL:

RADIANCE WITH HER FATHER

READ

At Radiance's request, Lyell H'arrant sat down next to her on the stage steps, and for half an hour, he talked about his scars. All the marks he'd received because he worked with fire.

Radiance liked scars. With so many healers in King's Barrow, most people didn't have scars. When someone *did* have a scar, it meant there was a story of some kind, and she liked stories very much. Lyell was a talented storyteller, and he had kept all his fire scars. He hadn't allowed a healer to take any of them away.

"Here," he said and showed her the thick, straight scar across the heel of his left hand. "One morning, very early, I tripped on a bucket and nearly killed myself on the side of my kiln. Barely managed to grab something in time, and of course that something ended up being as hot as the *sun*—"

Radiance laughed. She couldn't help it. His voice was funny, and she could tell why everyone liked him. He could probably read a book on mathematics, a very large one, and it would sound interesting because he was the one reading it. Everyone would laugh.

"Your mother heard me thrashing about. She came out of the room and—"

What did he just say?

He said those words like she'd heard them before, when she had never heard them. Not about *her* mother. Radiance stared and stared, and Lyell kept talking and didn't appear to notice that he'd said something remarkable.

"So your mother came out and said, 'What are you doing?' And I said, 'I had an idea, and I had to try it!' And she said, 'Whenever you have *ideas*, things always go wrong.' And I said, 'Well, it's three o'clock in the morning, and I know better than to disturb you. I am no fool, woman.' And *you*, Radiance..."

Lyell paused, and his gaze flicked over to her. "You were sleeping in your crib on the other side of the room. Yes, in the room with my kiln. We tried to give you a more proper place, but you simply wouldn't hear of it. You cried every time we moved your crib. This particular night as I shouted about fire, you woke up and started laughing. It was like you understood me and everything that had happened, and you laughed and laughed, and we had no idea why."

He tapped the scar on his hand. "*That* is the story of this scar. And a fine one it is too."

WRITING *EXERCISE*

The Bible says the Creator is a good Father, who loves his children and is gentle with them. He is tender the way a shepherd is, cradling the little lambs in his arms.

> *Like a shepherd He will tend His flock,*
> *In His arm He will gather the lambs*
> *And carry them in His bosom;*
> *He will gently lead the nursing ewes.*
> (Isa. 40:11)

Write a story based on Isaiah 40:11. Make your main character an artist, like Radiance's father, who knows what Ruwok is like. How would Ruwok speak to an artist? What would his voice sound like or how might he "appear" to an artist? Be creative!

Time: Write as much as you can in 15 minutes.

THE FIRE WRITER

Congratulations! You finished the book!

I hope you and your child enjoyed this companion guide and the opportunities it provided to hear God's voice in creative ways. His voice is like finding water in the desert. He loves your voice and your child's voice, and writing down his words refreshes the heart.

EVALUATING YOUR CHILD'S WORK

If you're using this companion guide as part of your homeschool curriculum, here are a few simple things to consider as you evaluate your child's writing.

How Is God Revealed in Your Child's Story?

The Lord can reveal himself in a story in a thousand different ways! He knows what will minister to someone's heart, and at times he may reveal himself through something small that doesn't necessarily speak to most people, but it does speak to those who need it.

When looking for God in a story, pay attention to metaphors, how a story makes you feel, what moves you even if you don't understand why, and what gives you hope. Here are a few ideas for how God might be revealed in your child's story:

- Good conquers evil.
- A father figure shows love to a child.
- Someone is adopted.
- There is a person/creature/element of light in darkness.
- Hope comes.
- Someone is redeemed, healed, made to feel welcome.
- God works according to abundant life, so any element of "abundant life" in a story could reveal him.

Discuss with your child how his or her story might reveal God. (Keep in mind this can be somewhat subjective.) Help your child to see how he or she might have heard and responded to God's leading during the writing process.

Always Praise Your Child for His or Her Creativity

Your encouragement can open the door of your child's heart. Even if a story is written poorly, with great exaggeration, or would never happen in real life, speak encouragement.

Depending on your child's age, you may or may not want to "correct" a storyline. Give your child the freedom to practice hearing God's voice through writing without the pressure to perform or follow all the "rules." If there is something you need to address, do so with epic kindness because writers are often sensitive.

When I wrote my first little story at eight years old, my parents responded so positively that I felt like I was good at writing, which made me want to keep going. Their support back then continues to play a role in what I'm writing today. A young child's story will often have obvious flaws, but certain things don't need to be discussed with a writer who is just starting out. The story doesn't have to be perfect right now. The main thing is that the child is interested in writing and wants to write. So encouragement is huge at this stage.

The Mechanics of Writing

Here are a few things to look for as you assess your child's understanding of grammar, punctuation, and sentence structure.

1. Does your child vary his or her sentence structure?

"The dog ran. The dog came to a fence. The dog jumped the fence. The dog ran some more."

If every sentence in your child's story follows the same pattern, try to introduce creative variance. Sentences can be rearranged to help draw readers into the story. Encourage your child to combine sentences and change up the flow. (But even here try to avoid making this sound like "correction.")

"The dog ran. When he reached a fence, he jumped over it and kept running."

If your child has trouble understanding how to do this, offer examples. Find children's books where the sentences are simple but creative, and go over them with your child.

2. Does your child understand subject-verb agreement?

"The dog and cat is coming with us."

A plural noun (the dog and cat) requires a plural verb (are). Train your child to recognize plural nouns and to double check the verb that follows them.

3. Are there any misplaced modifiers?

"I love to drink coffee with my cats first thing in the morning."

What? The cats are drinking coffee with you? Those are some amazing cats!

Even seasoned writers occasionally have misplaced modifiers, some of which can be pretty funny at times. Writers see the picture of what they're trying to say, but sometimes the words don't come out as clearly as the picture in their heads. Help your child to rearrange the words so the meaning is obvious and not confusing.

"I love to drink coffee first thing in the morning and watch my cats play on the rug."

4. Does your child use pronouns correctly?

"Me and Mom are going to the store."

The verb in a sentence acts like a fence, and certain words usually go on one side of the fence or the other. The pronoun *me* goes after the verb, while the pronoun *I* typically comes before it.

Also, it is considered polite to mention the other person first. So the corrected sentence would read like this:

"Mom and I are going to the store."

5. Are there any misspelled words?

Some people are naturally more gifted at spelling than others, but good spelling can be taught. Especially if your child consistently misspells a certain word, go over that word with the child until he or she starts to understand the correct way to spell it.

6. Does your child understand basic punctuation?

Basic punctuation includes periods, commas, question marks, exclamation points, and quotation marks. In the United States, most punctuation occurs *inside* the quotation marks. (A surprising number of writers don't realize this.)

"Did you hear the news? They said Billy's a finalist!"

"Do you think I need help with this project?"

7. Does your child know how to separate his or her story into paragraphs?

When young writers are first starting out, the entire story might be one long paragraph that goes on for three pages. Teach your child to break the story up into several different paragraphs, depending on the story's length. Dialogue usually starts a new paragraph, and when multiple characters speak back and forth, there may be several short paragraphs in a row.

"Who are you, sir?" she whispered, the words lost in all the fire. More than she loved fire, more than she loved water, she suddenly had to know.

"Someone who has waited a long time to be a main character in your story," he replied kindly.

And from that point forward, no one needed to explain anything else. She had no questions about who this man was. She looked into his fire eyes—the eyes of a deep blaze—and just knew.

Ruwok.

For here the earth breathes
— Shel Galen —
from his
History of Earth and Soil

www.ingramcontent.com/pod-product-compliance
Lightning Source LLC
Chambersburg PA
CBHW050455110426
42743CB00017B/3368